ALPHABET ART

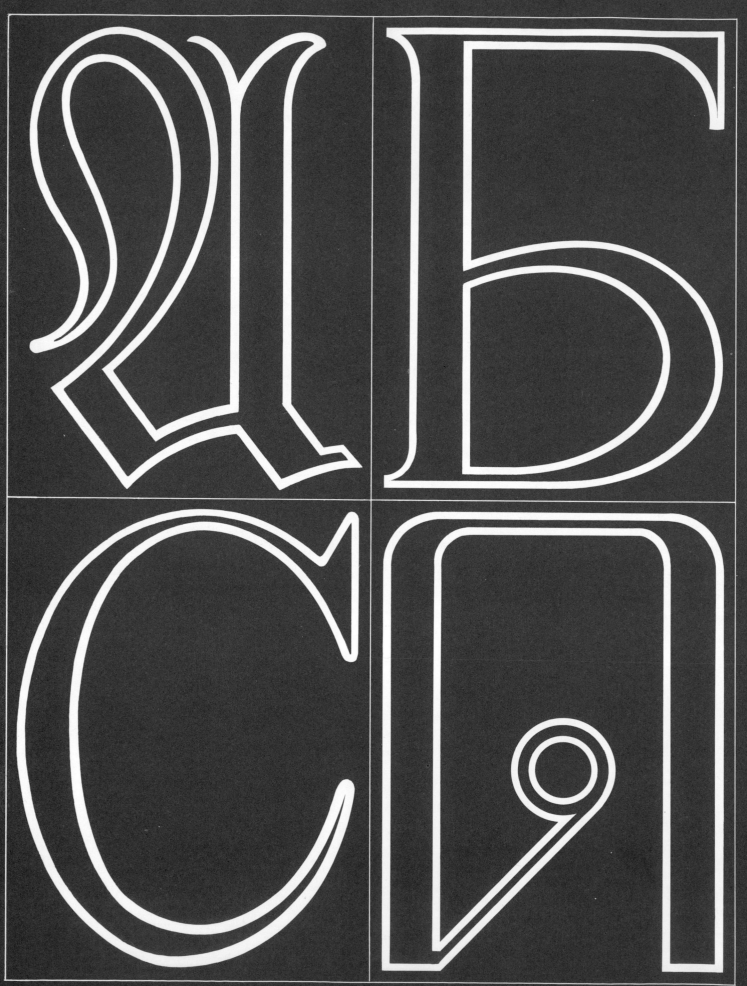

upper left, German A; *upper right*, Cyrillic B; *lower left*, Roman C; *lower right*, Thai D

ALPHABET ART
Thirteen ABCs from around the world

WRITTEN AND ILLUSTRATED BY
LEONARD EVERETT FISHER

FOUR WINDS PRESS   NEW YORK

For Marge

LIBRARY OF CONGRESS CATALOGING IN PUBLICATION DATA

FISHER, LEONARD EVERETT.
ALPHABET ART.

1. ALPHABETS.   2. LETTERING.   I. TITLE.
NK3600.F6   745.6′1   78-6148
ISBN 0-590-07520-9

PUBLISHED BY FOUR WINDS PRESS
A DIVISION OF SCHOLASTIC MAGAZINES, INC., NEW YORK, N.Y.
COPYRIGHT © 1978 BY LEONARD EVERETT FISHER
ALL RIGHTS RESERVED
PRINTED IN THE UNITED STATES OF AMERICA
LIBRARY OF CONGRESS CATALOG CARD NUMBER: 78-6148
2 3 4 5 82 81 80 79

ALPHABET ART

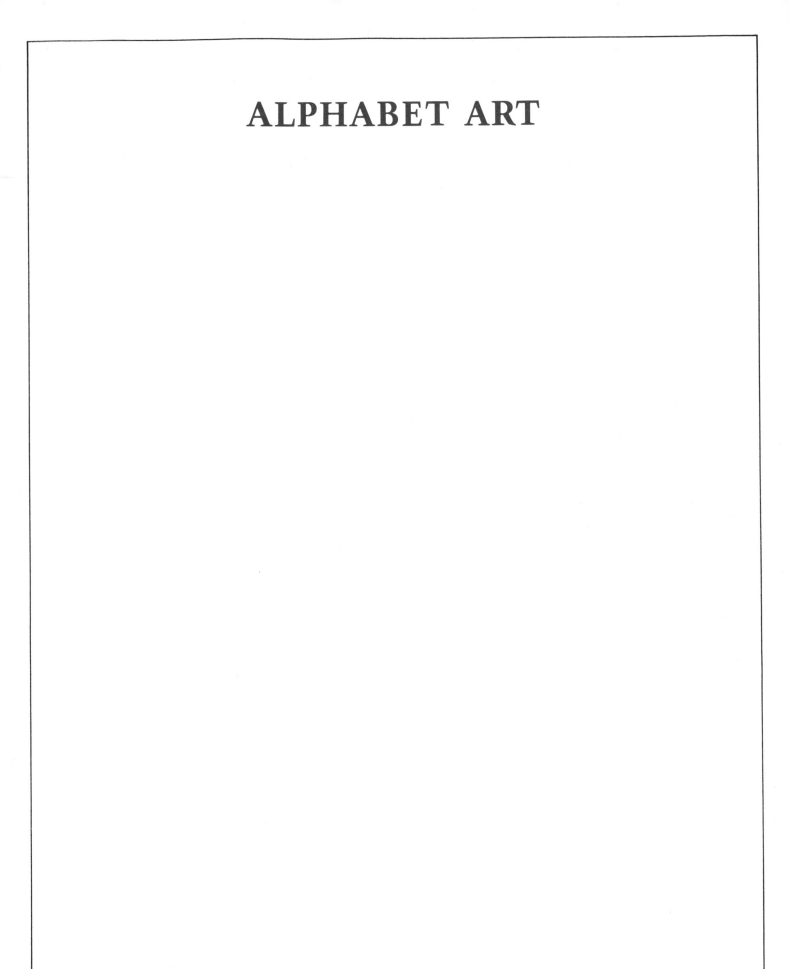

HIEROGLYPH
Egypt
c. 3000 B.C.

owl

CUNEIFORM
Sumeria
c. 2500 B.C.

bird

HIERATIC
Egypt
c. 1500 B.C.

owl

SINAI c. 1500 B.C.	PHOENICIAN c. 1000 B.C.	GREEK c. 800-400 B.C.	ROMAN c. A.D. 100	MODERN ENGLISH	SINAI c. 1500 B.C.	PHOENICIAN c. 1000 B.C.	GREEK c. 800-400 B.C.	ROMAN c. A.D. 100	MODERN ENGLISH
ox — aleph	ox — aleph	alpha	A	A	fish — nun	fish — nun	nu	N	N
house — beth	house — beth	beta	B	B	eye — ayin	eye — ayin	omicron	O	O
corner — gimel	corner — gimel	gamma	C	C	mouth — pe	mouth — pe	pi	P	P
	door — daleth	delta	D	D	knot — qoph	knot — qoph	koppa	Q	Q
praying man — he	window — he	epsilon	E	E	head — resh	head — resh	rho	R	R
hook — vau	hook — vau		F	F	teeth — shin	teeth — shin	sigma	S	S
			G	G	mark — tau	mark — tau	tau	T	T
braid — cheth	fence — cheth	eta	H	H					U
hand — yod	hand — yod	iota	I	I			upsilon	V — zeta	V
				J					W
palm of hand — kaph	palm of hand — kaph	kappa	K	K		support — sameth	chi	X	X
ox stick — lamed	ox stick — lamed	lambda	L	L				Y	Y
waters — mem	waters — mem	mu	M	M	weapon — zayin	weapon — zayin		Z	Z

THE ABCD OF LANGUAGE

Everyone knows what an alphabet is: a group of letters, characters, or symbols used to write or print words in a particular language.

ABCDEFGHIJKLMNOPQRSTUVWXYZ

or

abcdefghijklmnopqrstuvwxyz

is the alphabet of the English language—that set of upper- or lowercase letters used to create the words you are now reading. These letters are also used to print words in Spanish, French, Italian, and a variety of other languages.

Not everyone knows, however, the look of the characters the Indians of Bombay use to represent their ancient language; or, for that matter, those of the more recent alphabet of the Cherokee Indians of North America; or those of the Arabs, Chinese, Eskimos, Germans, Greeks, Irish, Japanese, Jews, Russians, Thais, and Tibetans. That is what this book is all about—the look of different alphabets of some non-English-speaking people in use around the modern world. These alphabets belong to varying cultural segments of the globe where ideas and events are expressed and communicated with sets of written or printed characters that are sometimes similar to but usually different from the standard English or Roman letters used to print the words on this page.

WHEN ALPHABETS BEGAN

History is a key word in the story of man's presence on planet Earth. History is recorded time—man's written account of his own activities and ideas. History began when man first gave an account of being here, there, everywhere; of doing this and that; of thinking how, why, and wherefore. Of course, man was on planet Earth long before recorded time, before history. Prehistoric man, unlike "his-

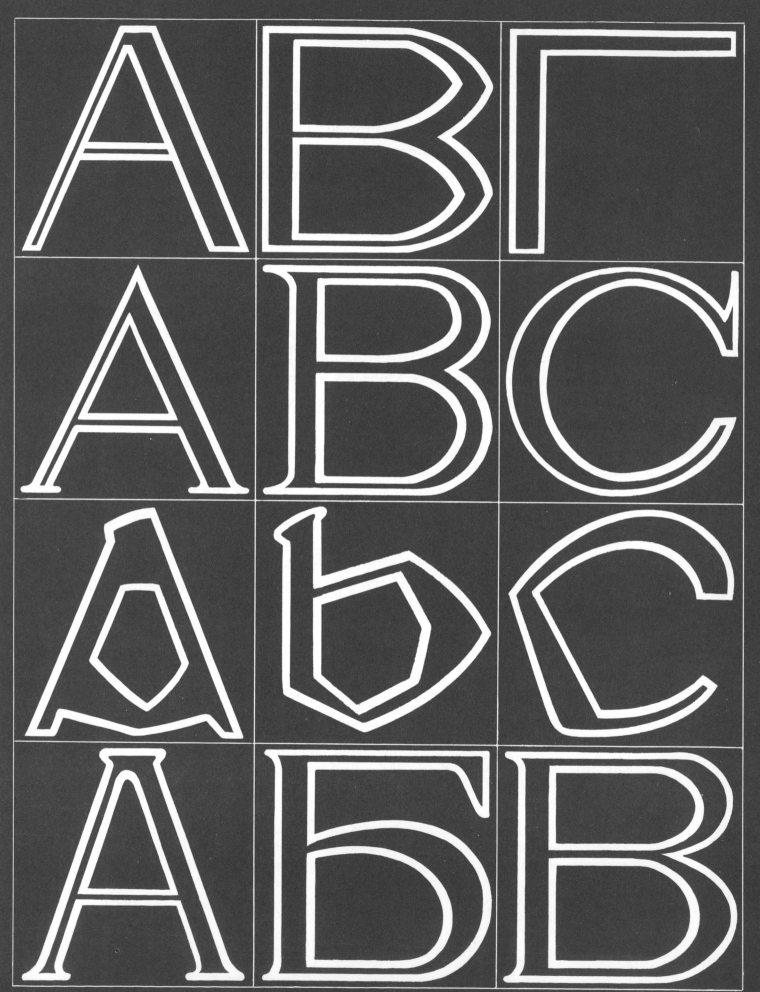

top to bottom: Greek A B C; Roman A B C; Gaelic A B C; Cyrillic A B C

THE ALPHABETS AND THEIR ILLUSTRATIVE INSCRIPTIONS

ARABIC
There is no God but God, and Mohammed is the prophet of God.

CHEROKEE
Cherokee

CHINESE
1978 The Year of the Horse

CYRILLIC
Bolshoi Theater, Moscow

ESKIMO
Hudson Bay Company

GAELIC
Music Festival of Ireland

GERMAN
The Festival of October

GREEK
Man, Myth, and Greece

HEBREW
In the beginning God created the heaven and the earth. (*Genesis 1:1*)

JAPANESE
Kibuki Theater of Japan

SANSKRIT
God speaks.

THAI
A Thai spirit

TIBETAN
O, the jewel in the lotus.

ARABIC

Rooted in Egyptian hieratic writing and Sinai and Phoenician letter-signs, Arabic alphabet characters have a graceful rhythm that seems to suggest a compelling motion. There is a flow of purpose and continuity to the letters that reflects the reach of an ancient but still vigorous Semitic people who are descended from the dim Biblical past of the Hebrew patriarch, Abraham of Ur.

Rising out of the hot, dry sand of the Arabian Peninsula in the southwest corner of Asia sometime after the fourth century A.D., the alphabet of Arabia quickly spread through the Middle East, along the neighboring coast of East Africa, and into Central Africa. By the eleventh century, Arab conquests had engulfed all of North Africa, Spain, Sicily, the Balkans, and Turkey. Arab culture had successfully dominated nearly the whole of the Mediterranean community. Aggressive Arab merchants, adventurers, and poets passed its religion, Islam, eastward along the great trade routes to the Orient, as far as the Philippine Islands. Arab architecture, decoration, science, medicine, mathematics, and literature—chiefly the *Koran*, the sacred writings of Islam in which the word of God, Allah, was revealed to the prophet, Mohammed—flowed everywhere the followers of Islam introduced Arab civilization.

Finally, Arab vitality subsided during the thirteenth century as others emerged to assert their cultural integrity. The forces of Arabia withdrew. The empire shrank. Yet the religious power of Islam remained to shape the largest bloc of "believers" in the world. Today, some five hundred million Moslems—those who submit to the doctrines of Islam but who are not necessarily Arabian or even speak everyday Arabic—are bound together by a common scripture, the *Koran*, and by the sharp presence of that book's original and widely used language and alphabet—Arabic.

ا A *alif* (silent)	ب B *be* (b)
ت T *te* (t)	ث *the* (th)
ج J *jim* (j)	ح H *he* (h)
خ *khe* (kh)	د D *dal* (d)
ذ *dhal* (dl)	ر R *re* (r)
ز Z *ze* (z)	س S *sin* (s)
ش *shin* (sh)	ص S *sad* (s)

ض dad (th)	ط T ta (t)
ظ Z za (z)	ع ayn (silent)
غ ghayn (gh)	ف F fe (f)
ق Q qaf (k)	ك K kaf (k)
ل L lam (l)	م M mim (m)
ن N nun (n)	ه H he (h)
و W waw (w)	ى Y ye (y)

D	S	W	W	Ⴑ	Ө
A (ah or uh)	ga ka	ha	la	ma	na hna nah
R	Ⱶ	Ⴒ	Ꮛ	Ᏸ	Ⴥ
E (aee or eh)	ge	he	le	me	ne
T	Ᏹ	Ꮧ	Ꮅ	Ᏺ	Ꮒ
I (eee or ih)	gi	hi	li	mi	ni
Ꮥ	Ꭺ	Ꮎ	G	Ꮙ	Z
O (aw or ah)	go	ho	lo	mo	no
Ꮕ	Ꭻ	Ꮪ	Ꮃ	Ꮉ	Ꮕ
U (oo or uh)	gu	hu	lu	mu	nu
i	E	Ꮯ	Ꮈ	Ꮊ	Ꮕ
V (uh)	gv	hv	lv		nv

qua	sa / s	da / ta	dla / tla	tsa	wa	ya
que	se	de / te	tle	tse	we	ye
qui	si	di / ti	tli	tsi	wi	yi
quo	so	do	tlo	tso	wo	yo
quu	su	du	tlu	tsu	wu	yu
quv	sv	dv	tlv	tsv	wv	yv

CHINESE

Scholars are not sure when the Chinese system of writing began. Some say that Chinese characters first appeared between 3000 and 3500 years ago. Others think that the system began earlier. The letters or characters themselves probably developed from picture representations of objects and ideas—a circle for the sun, a crescent for the moon, and so on. Whatever the case, Chinese is one of the oldest continuously used languages in the world. Today it is spoken by at least seven hundred million people.

There are countless variations of spoken Chinese, which are sometimes so different that an individual speaking one dialect may not be understood by someone speaking another dialect. This is not true of the written language, which is the same for everyone.

The writing of Chinese was—and to a great extent, still is—a difficult, complex affair. There is no true alphabet for classical Chinese, no simple order of letters with which one can spell every Chinese word. Instead, Chinese is a syllabary made up of some ten thousand characters that represent complete ideas, syllables, sounds, or whole words. Only the most highly educated scholars can hope to master the full range of Chinese as it has been written through the ages. Moderately educated Chinese can get along with about half that number, or five thousand characters. Those who are acquainted with three thousand or fewer characters are only partially literate. The remainder of the population can hardly read classical Chinese, if at all.

For nearly one hundred years, the various Chinese governments have been encouraging the simplification and standardization of written Chinese to reduce the country's illiteracy. Most of these efforts have included the transcribing of Chinese sounds into Roman letters. On the following two pages is *Pin-yin*, one of the more popularized systems that relates Chinese *phonetic* or sound symbols to Roman letters or groups of letters. These characters can be combined variously in vowel-consonant-syllabic patterns representing the full spectrum of modern spoken Chinese.

B *po* (b)

N *ne* (n)

Q *ch'i* (ch)

P *p'o* (p)

L *le* (l)

X *hsi* (ch)

M *mo* (m)

G *ko* (g)

Z *tzu* (ds)

F *fo* (f)

K *k'o* (k)

C *ts'u* (ts)

D *te* (d)

H *ho* (ch)

S *ssu* (s)

T *t'e* (t)

J *chi* (j)

chih (zh)

ㄔ *ch'ih* (ch)	ㄜ E *e* (uh)	ㄢ *an* (an)
ㄕ *shih* (sh)	ㄛ O *o* (oo)	ㄤ *ang* (ang)
ㄖ R *jih* (r)	ㄩ U *yu* (yu)	ㄟ *ei* (aee)
ㄧ I or Y *i* (y)	ㄦ *erh* (er)	ㄣ *en* (un)
ㄨ W *wu* (w)	ㄞ *ai* (ai)	ㄥ *eng* (eng)
ㄚ A *ia* (ah)	ㄠ *ao* (ow)	ㄡ *yu* (oh)

CYRILLIC

In 863 A.D., two Greek brothers, Cyril and Methodius, were sent west from Constantinople, the heart of the Byzantine empire, to Moravia, a hilly region in present-day central Czechoslovakia. Their task was to convert the pagan Moravian Slavs to Christianity. Their only tool was an alphabet derived from Greek but which they had altered, refined, and completed two years before. Cyril and Methodius had revised the alphabet to record the language of the Moravians. Ultimately, they hoped to teach the Moravians to read in their own tongue the Bible and other religious writings which Cyril and Methodius had translated from the original Latin, Greek, and possibly Hebrew or Aramaic.

The brothers were enormously successful. Despite fierce objections of neighboring German Christians, who viewed the conversion of any Slav by non-Roman churchmen as a threat both to the Church and to themselves, the Moravians became Christians. Cyril and Methodius were hailed as "Apostles to the Slavs." Eventually, they were elevated to sainthood, and the alphabet, Cyrillic, was named after one of them.

Not all Slavic people use the Cyrillic alphabet, however. Poles, Czechs, Slovaks, and Croatians, for example, use standard Roman letters. Their early history fell under the spell of the West—the Church of Rome—rather than the East—the Empire of Byzantium.

Later, eastern missionaries spread the Cyrillic alphabet among the Serbs, Bulgars, and other Slavic tribes. In time Cyrillic found its way into the vast land mass of Russia. There, today, more than two hundred million people speaking at least one hundred different languages communicate nationally in Cyrillic. The official language of the Union of Soviet Socialist Republics is Russian, and it is visually expressed in the alphabet developed by Saints Cyril and Methodius.

А (ae)

Б (b)

В (v)

Г (g)

D (d)

(ye)

(zh)

Z (z)

I (ee)

I (ee)

K (k)

L (l)

M (m)

N (n)

O (oh)

P (p)

Р R (r)	**С** S (s)	**Т** T (t)	**У** Y (oo)
Ф F (f)	**Х** (kh)	**Ц** (ts)	**Ч** (ch)
Ш (sh)	**Щ** (shch)	**Ъ** (indicates non-palatalization of preceding consonant)	**Ы** (ee)
Ь (indicates palatalization of preceding consonant)	**Э** E (eh)	**Ю** (eu)	**Я** (yae)

ESKIMO

The Eskimo language belongs to a family of languages called *Eskimo-Aleut*. These languages are spoken in the arctic climates of Greenland, Canada, Alaska, and Eastern Siberia. Eskimo itself is a single language having several dialects. One of these dialects—*Inupik*—is the tongue of the Canadian Greenland and Eastern Alaskan Eskimos. Inupik Eskimo can be written or printed in either standard English letters or Eskimo letters—a group of angles, triangles, lines, arcs, and circles vaguely reminiscent of Greek.

Like Chinese and Cherokee, the Eskimo "alphabet" is not a true alphabet. It is a syllabary, a set of symbols denoting sound combinations of the Eskimo language. Curiously, these Eskimo letters were not meant for the Eskimos at all. They were designed originally for the Cree Indians of Canada to enable them to read the Bible. The Crees apparently never reacted to their custom-tailored "alphabet." They either failed to grasp the usefulness of it or else rejected the idea for other reasons.

In 1878, the Reverend Edmund J. Peck of the Church Missionary Society introduced the discarded "alphabet" to the Canadian Eskimos. It took a long time for the shy and isolated Eskimos of the Canadian Far North to adopt the written symbols for their own—but adopt them they did!

In 1953, the Canadian government, recognizing the connection between the widespreading use of the Eskimo syllabary and the distinct Eskimo culture within its borders, published, for the first time, an Eskimo-language magazine. Since that time the Eskimo publishing program has been a fact of Canadian life. Such works as *Q-Book*, a publication in Eskimo by the government of Canada, keeps the Eskimos informed about ideas, events, and practical technology of the modern world in their own language and "alphabet."

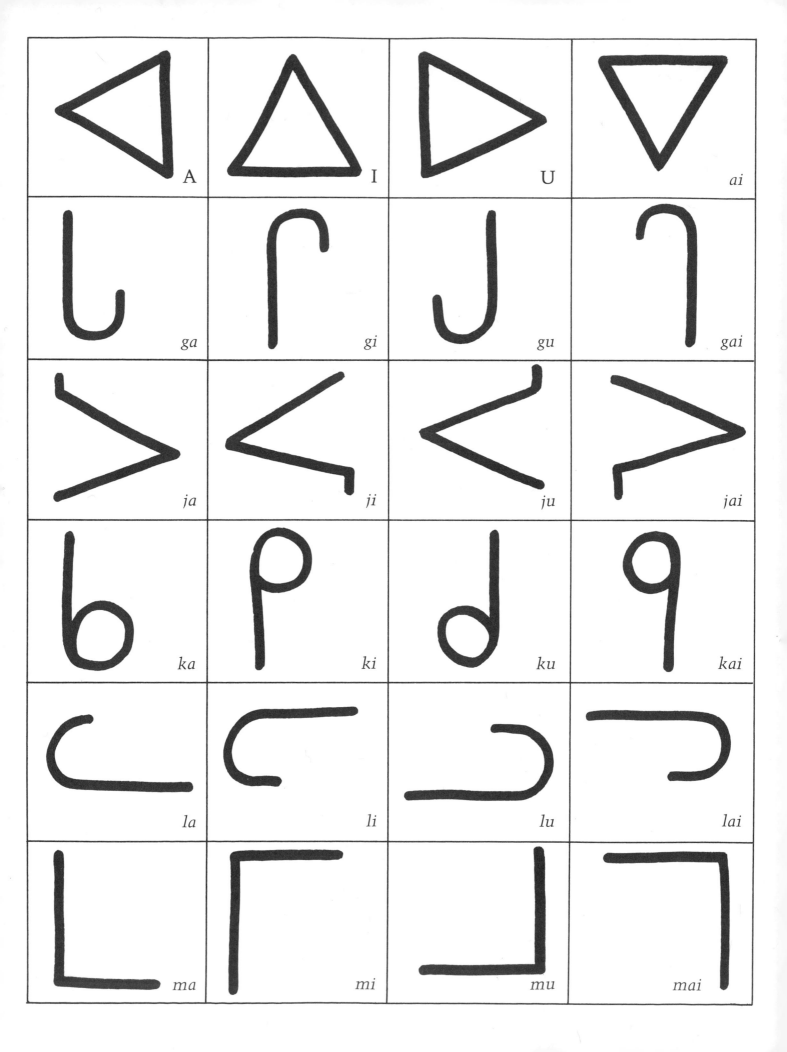

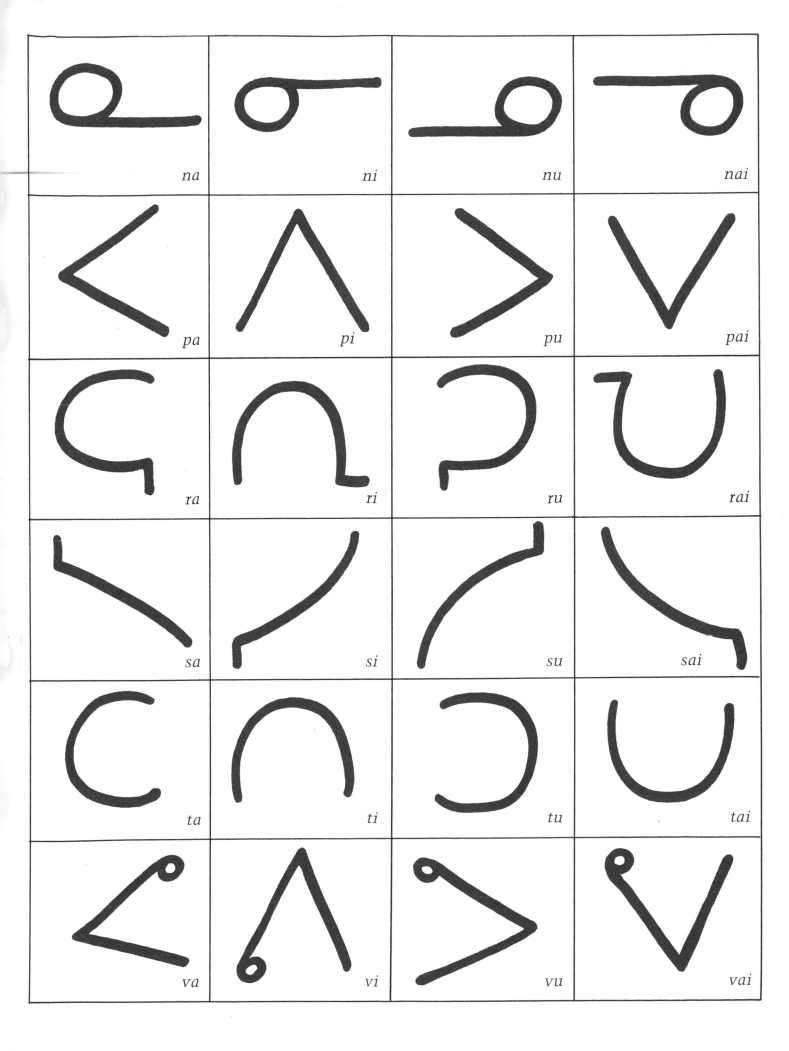

na	*ni*	*nu*	*nai*
pa	*pi*	*pu*	*pai*
ra	*ri*	*ru*	*rai*
sa	*si*	*su*	*sai*
ta	*ti*	*tu*	*tai*
va	*vi*	*vu*	*vai*

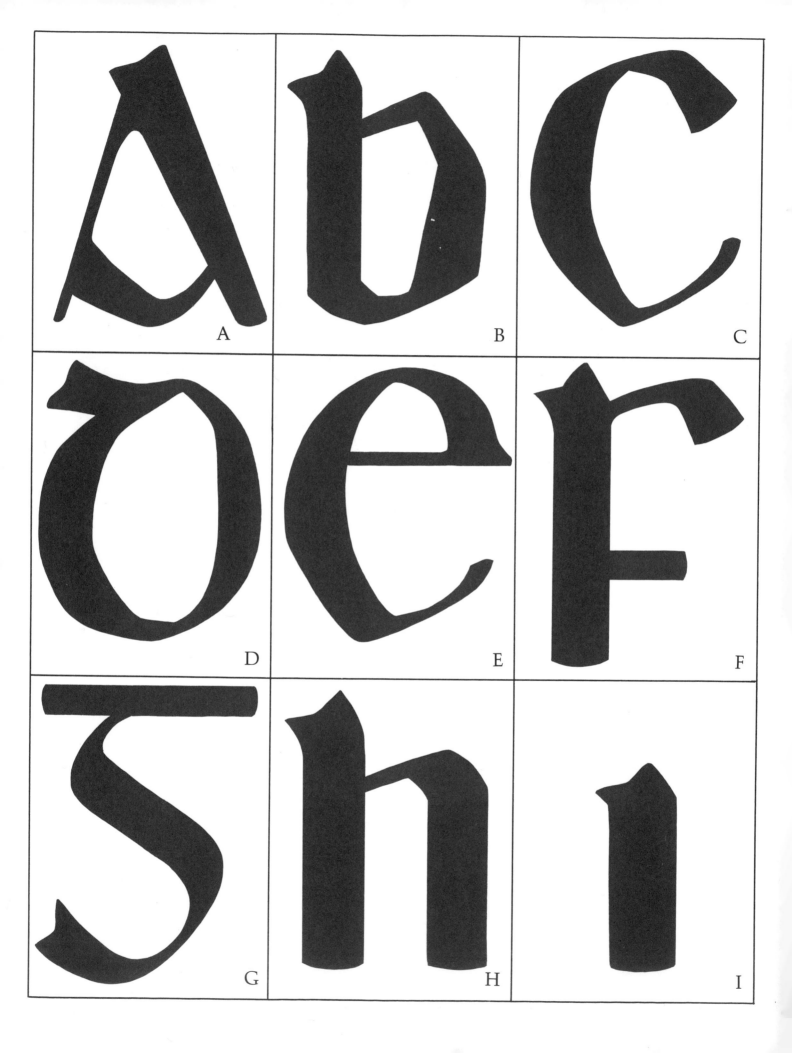

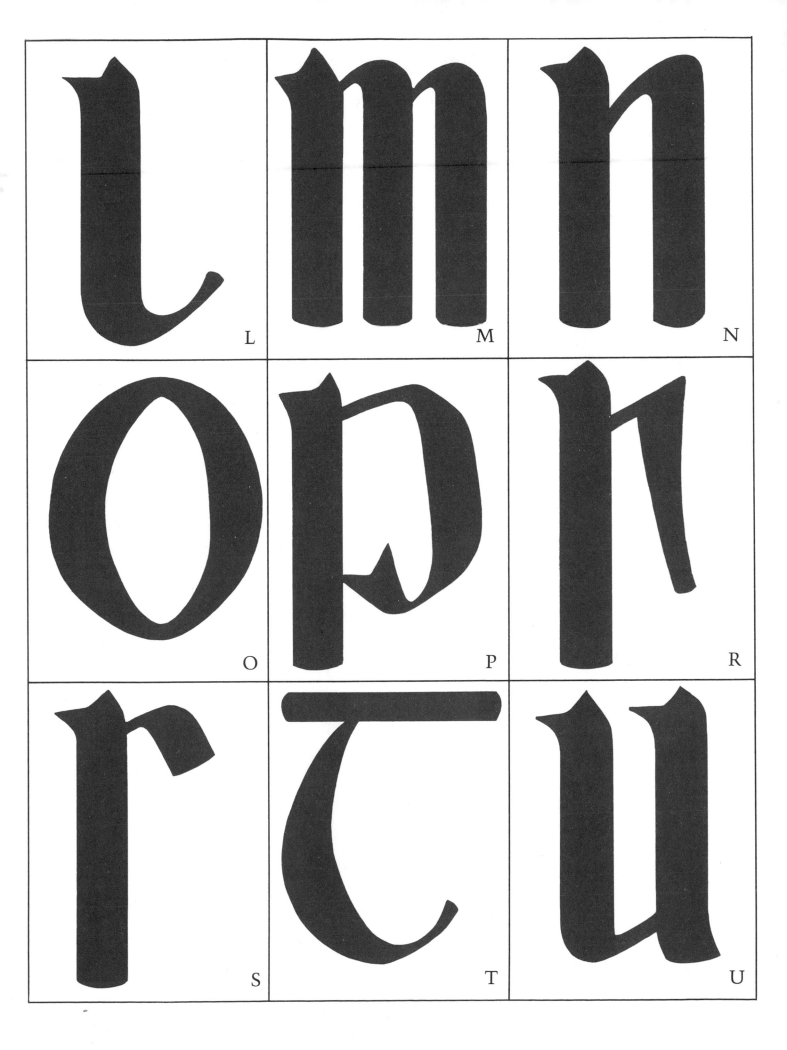

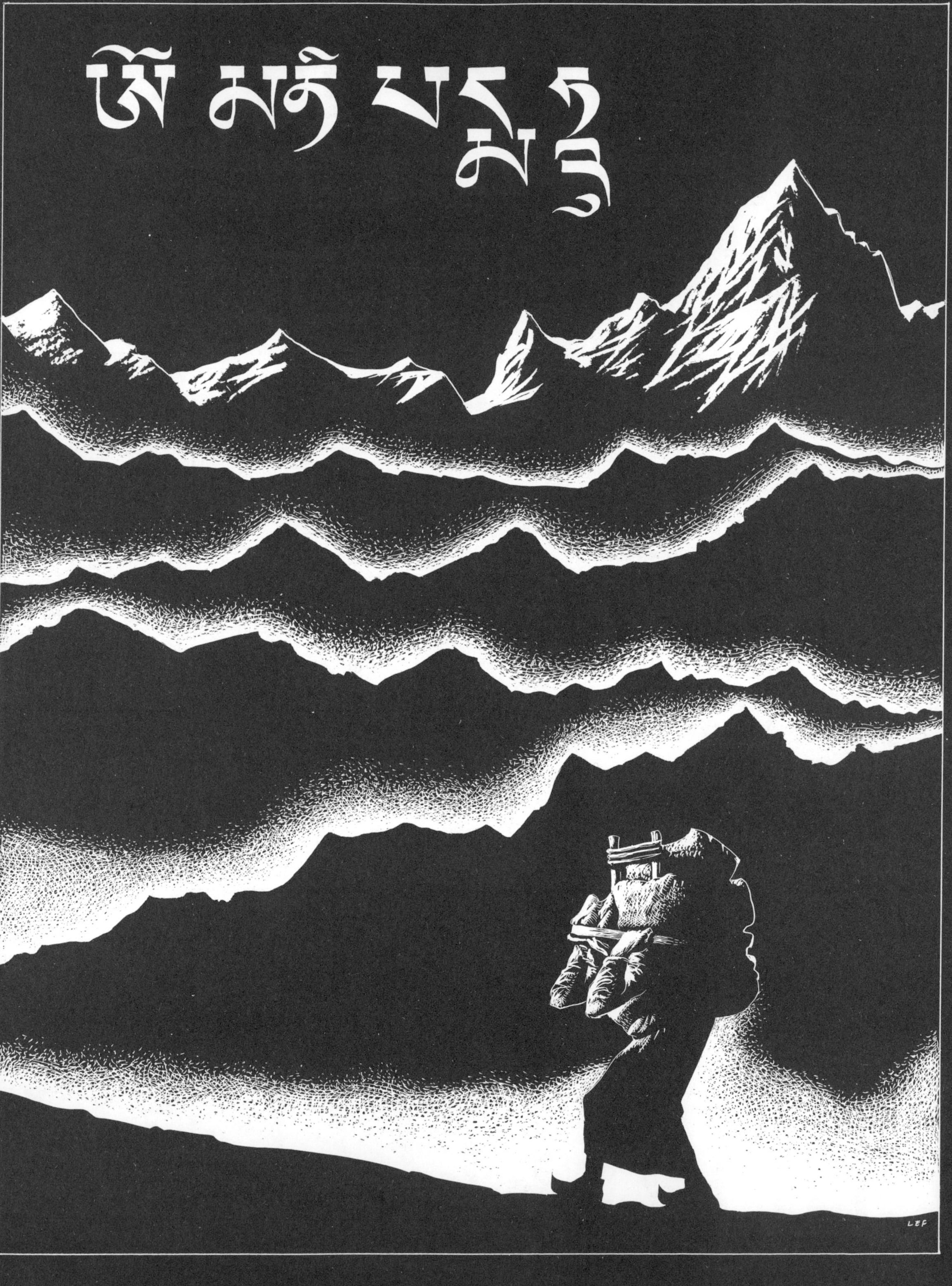
ཨོ མ ཎི པ དྨ ཧུ
LEF

der OKTOBERFEST

GERMAN

Like most languages, spoken German has variations. Basically, however, there are two major branches of the German language today: Low German and High German. Low German is the principal dialect of northern Germany. It is linked to English, Dutch, Flemish, and Afrikaan since all of these languages have a common beginning in an earlier Germanic tongue. High German, on the other hand, is the dialect of southern Germany, Austria, and northern Switzerland. Spoken Yiddish, Pennsylvania Dutch, and Alsatian are related to High German.

Whatever the dialect, the written or printed form of the language is High German. And the design of the alphabet letters—an alphabet rooted in the Phoenician-Greek-Roman families—continues the Gothic tradition of medieval Europe from whence it originated some one thousand years ago.

"Gothic" was a derisive term coined by later Italian esthetes to describe what they considered to be crude and vulgar artistic styles of northern Europe, chiefly of Germany. Regardless, the thick and energetic style of German alphabet letters clearly reflects a vigorous time that marked the emergence of German culture. Also called the *Dark Ages*, the Gothic period was a time of cathedral building, superstition, crusades, and plagues. Yet, the Gothic period spawned towns, trade, commerce, the middle class, craft guilds, universities, learning, civic pride, and a tradition of romantic love. Moreover, it heralded the coming of the intellectual reawakening of western man, the Renaissance. By its continuous use, this non-Romanized German alphabet seems to stand alone in symbolizing man's parallel natures, his ignorance and enlightenment, so sharply delineated during the Gothic period.

A *ah*

E *ah* (eh)

B *bay*

C *tsay*

tsay-*hah* (kh)

D *day*

E *ay* (eh or ai)

F *eff*

G *gay* (g or kh)

H *hah*

I *ee*

K *kah*

L *ell*

M *em*

N *en*

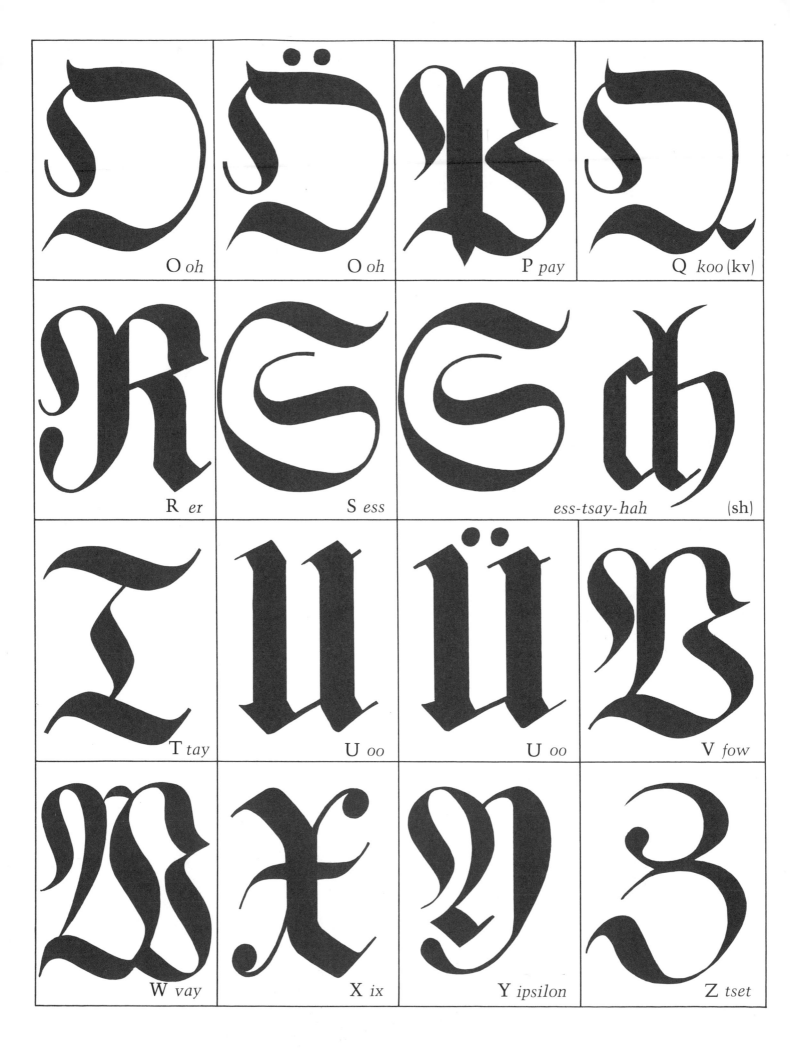

O *oh*

O *oh*

P *pay*

Q *koo* (kv)

R *er*

S *ess*

ess-tsay-hah (sh)

T *tay*

U *oo*

U *oo*

V *fow*

W *vay*

X *ix*

Y *ipsilon*

Z *tset*

ΑΝΘΡΩΠΟΣ ΜΙΘΟΣ
ΚΑΙ ΕΛΛΑΣ

GREEK

One of the more glittering moments in the history of the world occurred, roughly, during a one-hundred-year period called the Golden Age of Greece, or the Classical Period. That era—c. 499–399 B.C.—began with the birth of Pericles, an enlightened politician who made Athens the intellectual and cultural force of the ancient world. It ended with the death of Socrates, the Athenian philosopher condemned to die for daring to heighten man's awareness of himself in contradiction to the glorification of the state. Between these two events, an alliance of rival Greek city-states led by Athens kept Persian armies from overrunning Europe and went on to create a manner of life which still serves as a model of civilized thought and action.

During this fifth century before the coming of Christianity—among olive groves shading dazzling sunlight, on countless islands sparkling in the bluest sea—the ancient Greeks practiced democracy, created architectural wonders and stunning sculpture, explored the sciences, perfected the drama, wrote poetry, philosophy and history, and refined a five-hundred-year-old alphabet (see page 6).

As previously noted, the word "alphabet" originated with the Greeks (see pages 8–9). Some early Greeks, the Dorians, adapted Phoenician and other Mediterranean characters about 1000 B.C. They added vowels and otherwise began a process of change that produced a Greek set of letters. Within two hundred years, Homer used these letters to write his accounts of the Trojan Wars and the wanderings of Odysseus—*The Iliad* and *The Odyssey*. Ensuing Greek colonization spread the Greek alphabet from Spain to India, forming an effective base for the creation of newer and different alphabets, chiefly in the Western world. As an indication of the wide respect for Greek scholarship and civilization, Greek was the written language of learned people everywhere until c. 500 A.D.

The alphabet shown on the following pages is modern Greek. It is not altogether that different from the alphabet of Pericles and his erudite contemporaries.

A *alpha* (ah)

B *beta* (b)

G *gamma* (g)

D *delta* (d)

E *epsilon* (eh)

Z *zeta* (dz)

H *eta* (ey)

theta (th)

I *iota* (ee)

K *kappa* (k)

L *lambda* (l)

M *mu* (m)

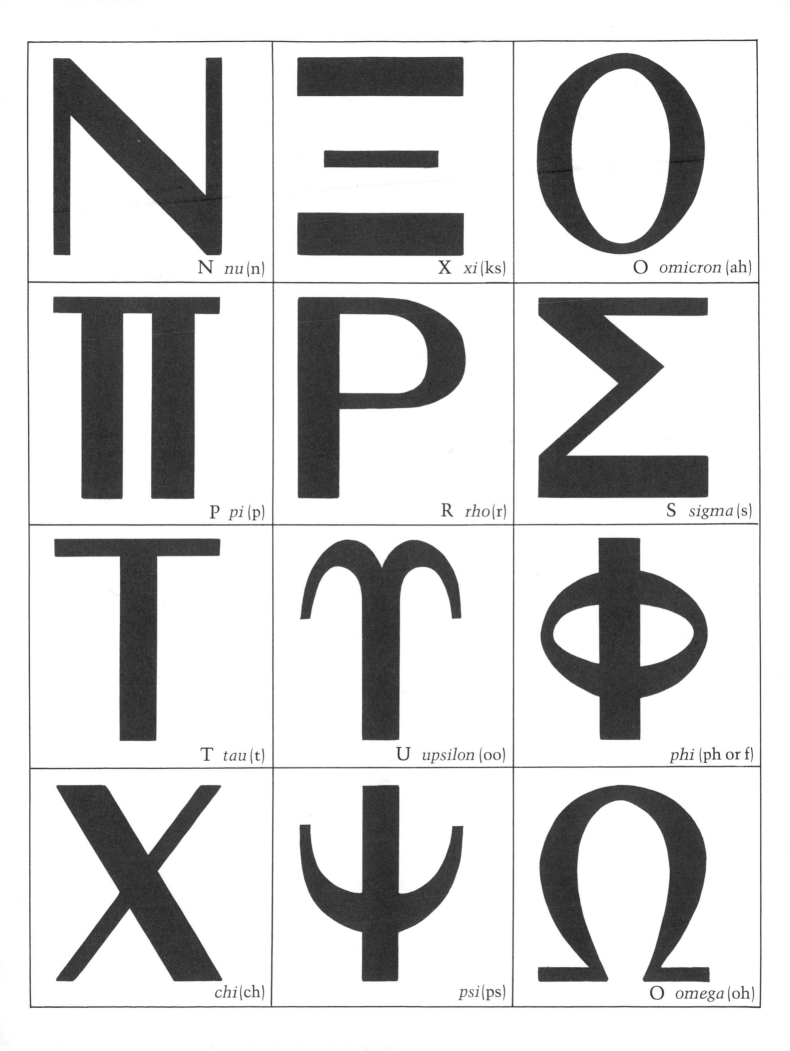

N *nu* (n)

X *xi* (ks)

O *omicron* (ah)

P *pi* (p)

R *rho* (r)

S *sigma* (s)

T *tau* (t)

U *upsilon* (oo)

phi (ph or f)

chi (ch)

psi (ps)

O *omega* (oh)

בְּרֵאשִׁית בָּרָא אֱלֹהִים אֵת הַשָּׁמַיִם וְאֵת הָאָרֶץ:

HEBREW

About four thousand years ago, a man named Abraham, his wife Sarah, his father Terah, and Lot, his nephew, left the Babylonian city of Ur and settled in southern Turkey. There, Terah died, and Abraham moved on after having begun a series of talks with God. God promised Abraham "the Hebrew" ("one from across the river"), and his descendants, land and survival in return for absolute faith in Him. Abraham agreed. Eventually, he went to Canaan—present-day Israel—the land God had promised him. Here, he made a binding contract with God, a Covenant. In time he fathered two sons: Ishmael, the child of Sarah's Egyptian maid, Hagar, and Isaac, born to Sarah in her old age, as God had foretold. Ishmael, rejected by God as Abraham's heir, was sent into the desert, destined, according to Moslem tradition, to seed a new people—the Arabs. Isaac was declared by God to be the heir upon whom would devolve the keeping of the Covenant and from whom would descend that branch of Abraham's relatives chosen by God to perpetuate the Covenant—the Jews.

This simple account of a complex story originated in the *Old Testament*, a collection of "books" written in Hebrew over a one-thousand-year period. The bulk of the *Old Testament* was written and revised between c. 1200–400 B.C. It is the most influential book in the world—the glue of Jewish life, the wellspring of Christianity, the genealogical spark of Islam. For twenty-five centuries now, Jews around the world have continued to read in the original Hebrew, almost daily, the *Torah*, the first five books of the *Old Testament*, reminding themselves of their responsibilities in keeping the four-thousand-year-old Covenant with God.

The Hebrew language and alphabet of today are not far removed from that of the *Old Testament*. Both the Hebrew language and alphabet are closely related to the earliest Egyptian, Sinai, and Phoenician tongues and writings. One of the oldest continuously used languages in human history, Hebrew is the language of the modern state of Israel and of Jewish religious institutions the world over.

A *aleph* (usually silent)

B *beth* (b)

V *veth* (v)

G *gimel* (g)

D *daleth* (d)

H *heh* (h)

V *vav* (v)

Z *zayin* (z)

kheth (kh)

T *teth* (t)

Y *yod* (y)

K *kaph* (k)

(final form used at end of a word)

K *khaph* (kh) (variation of kaph usually not included in alphabet)

(final form used at end of a word)

L *lamedh* (l)

M *mem* (m)

M *mem* (m) (final form used at end of a word)

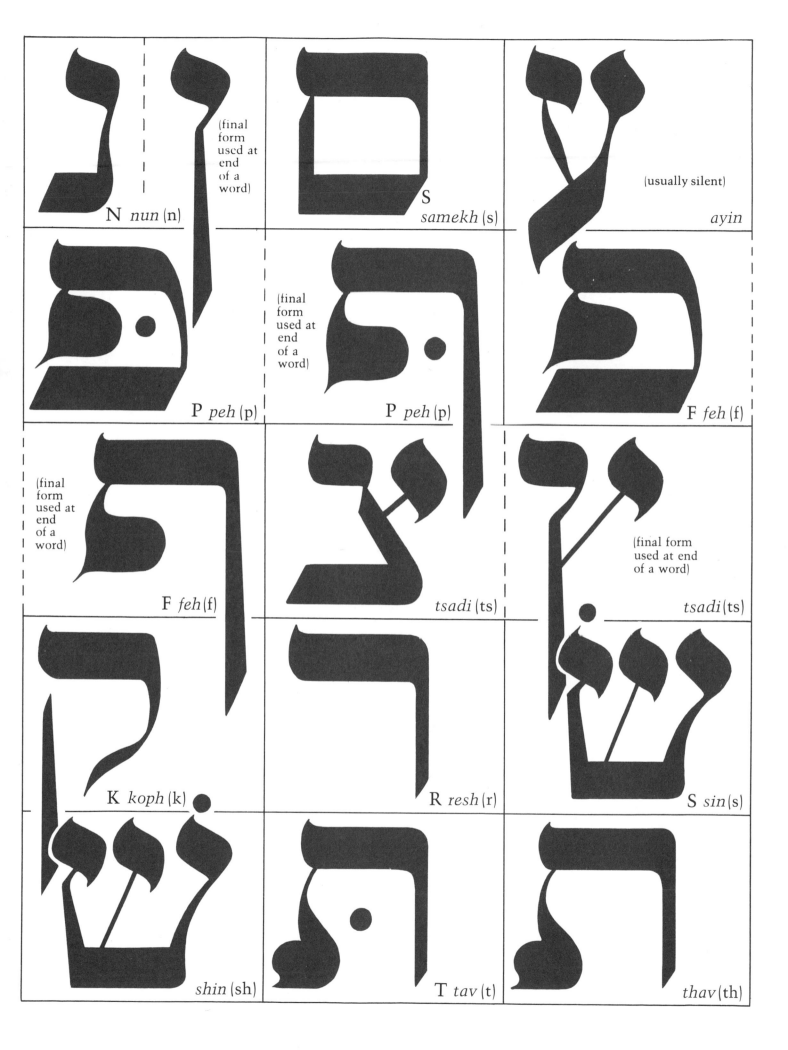

N *nun* (n) (final form used at end of a word)

S *samekh* (s)

ayin (usually silent)

P *peh* (p)

P *peh* (p) (final form used at end of a word)

F *feh* (f)

F *feh* (f) (final form used at end of a word)

tsadi (ts)

tsadi (ts) (final form used at end of a word)

K *koph* (k)

R *resh* (r)

S *sin* (s)

shin (sh)

T *tav* (t)

thav (th)

歌舞伎 日本

JAPANESE

Like Chinese, the configuration of Japanese alphabetical characters has no historical connection to the Sinai-Phoenician-Greek origins of Western alphabets. However, the Japanese writing system is less intricate than that of Chinese. Basing their writing system on classical Chinese and the thousands of Chinese letter-syllable symbols, the Japanese evolved several simpler approaches to their written language.

Until the mid-sixth century A.D., the Japanese had no written language of note. In 552 A.D., Chinese Buddhist priests came to Japan and introduced Buddhism and the Chinese writing system to the Japanese. Over the following one-hundred-sixty years, the Japanese, using Chinese characters, busily chronicled their earliest history, the *Kojiki*, which had been until then an oral history. They also wrote their first major poetical works, *Man-Yoshu*, in Chinese.

During the eleventh century A.D., Japanese scholars began to simplify the complex Chinese system of writing to better fit their more practical nature. They developed a variety of syllabaries, or *kana*, whose characters more clearly represented Japanese sounds and visual design. They also began to reduce the vast numbers of Chinese characters to a more manageable number.

Two such syllabaries, *Hiragana* and *Katakana*, are in constant use in present-day Japan. Hiragana represents ordinary writing. Katakana—the syllabary shown on the following pages—is an Italic style used for emphasis. *Kanamajiri*—"everyday" Japanese, shown in the illustration—combines Hiragana and Katakana with Chinese characters, which, according to Japanese scholars, is an unnecessary complication. Thus, an attempt is being made in modern Japan to Romanize Japanese with standard English letters.

	M	N	S	Z	P	B
A	ア	マ	ナ	サ	ザ	パ	バ
I	イ	ミ	ニ	シ	ジ	ピ	ビ
U	ウ	ム	ヌ	ス	ズ	プ	ブ
E	エ	ノ	ネ	セ	ゼ	ペ	ベ
O	オ	モ	ノ	ソ	ゾ	ポ	ボ
UN	ン						

T	D	K	G	Y	R	H	W
タ	ダ	カ	ガ	ヤ	ラ	ハ	ワ
チ	ヂ	キ	ギ	イ	リ	ヒ	キ
ツ	ヅ	ク	グ	ユ	ル	フ	ウ
テ	デ	ケ	ゲ	エ	レ	ヘ	エ
ト	ド	コ	ゴ	ヨ	ロ	ホ	ヲ

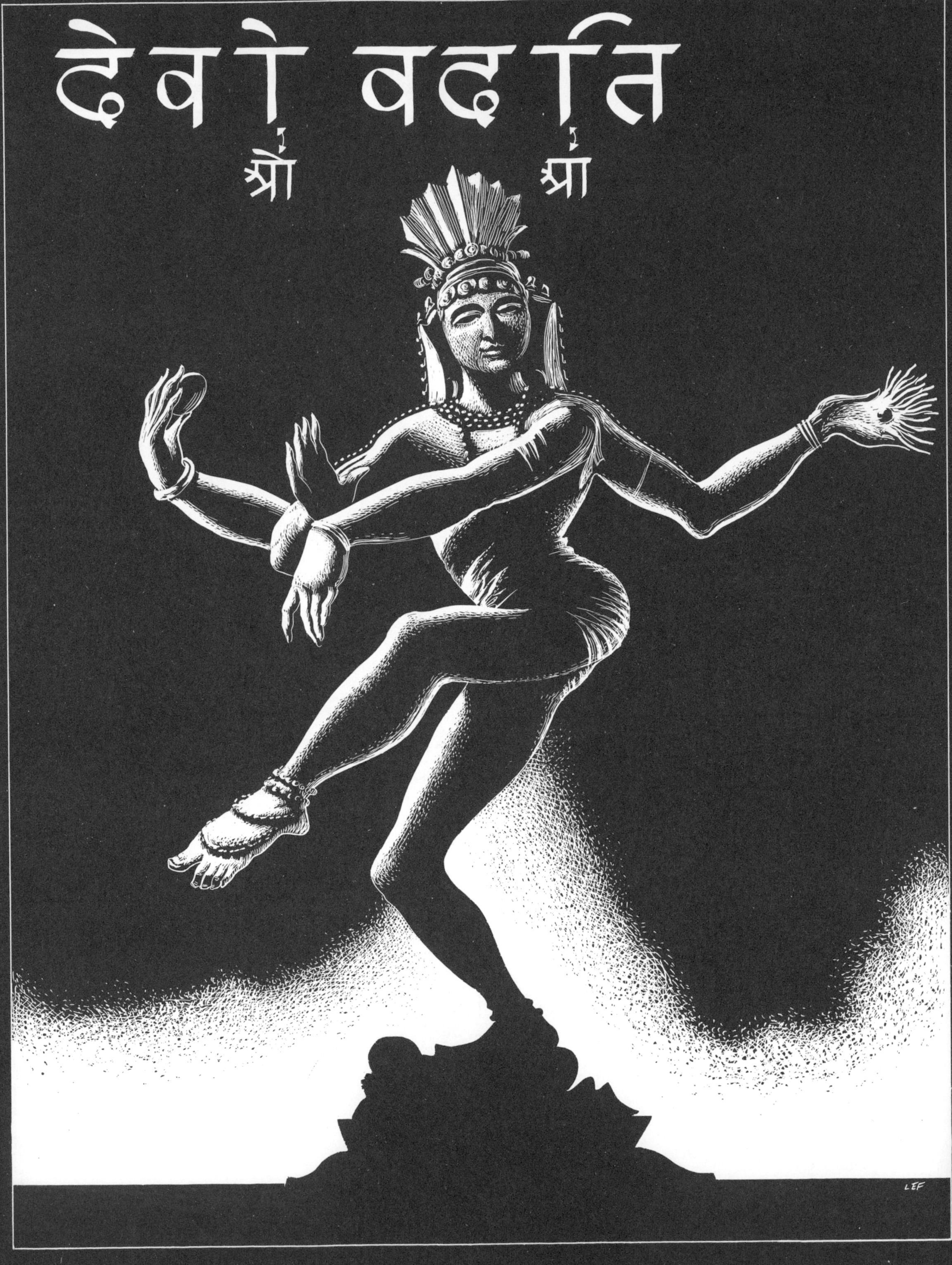
LEF

SANSKRIT

No one on the crowded Indian subcontinent of Asia today speaks Sanskrit casually. In fact, no one has used the ancient language conversationally for the past two thousand years. Hindi, Bengali, Marathi, Gujarati, Punjabi, and a variety of other tongues, all descended from Sanskrit, are the languages of the subcontinent.

Yet, far from being absolutely "dead," Sanskrit still serves the world's approximately 435 million Hindus—followers of India's "Eternal Religion." The word *Sanskrit* means "perfect" or "pure" in an older form of the language. As such, Sanskrit is the venerated literary language of modern Hinduism. The very roots of Hindu belief, custom, and culture are contained in timeless books written in Sanskrit.

The earliest known form of Sanskrit, *Vedic Sanskrit*, first appeared some thirty-five hundred years ago. It was derived from Egyptian hieratic writing, the writing of the priests. Over the next thirteen hundred years, from *c.* 1500–200 B.C., a period corresponding with the rise and decline of classical Greece, Vedic was the language of the *Vedas*, the most holy scriptures of Hinduism. Following that era of "Divine Knowledge," and for another thirteen hundred years—*c.* 200 B.C.–1100 A.D.—a more profane, or nonsacred, Hindu literature developed. Much of this was in verse. With this secular literature came an altered Sanskirt, classical Sanskrit, and an alphabet called *Devanagari* ("writing of the Gods"), shown on the following pages. (In the illustration, where two forms of the same letter are given, the bottom one is used when the letter appears by itself as an initial or when writing the alphabet.)

Today, Sanskrit is used to read the holy books of Hinduism and the great epic and lyric literature of the Hindu past, continuing an ancient, unbroken tradition among Hindus. Also it is the parent alphabet of a number of Asian alphabets (i.e., Thai and Tibetan). But more importantly, its literary presence is the cultural bond of Hinduism.

A *akara* (uh) A *akara* (ah) I *ikara* (ih) I *ikara* (ee)

U *ukara* (oo) U *ukara* (eu) R *rkara* (r) R *rkara* (r)

L *lkara* (l) L *lkara* (l) E *ekara* (a) *aikara* (ai)

O *okara* (oh) *aukara* (ow) K *kakara* (k) *khakara* (kh)

G *gakara* (g) *ghakara* (gh) N *nakara* (ng) *chakara* (ch)

chakara (tch) J *jakara* (j) *jhakara* (dge) N *nakara* (ny)

T *takara* (t)	*thakara* (th)	D *dakara* (d)	*dhakara* (dh)
N *nakara* (n)	L *lhakara* (l)	T *takara* (t't)	*thakara* (th)
D *dakara* (t'h)	*dhakara* (d'h)	*nakara* (n)	P *pakara* (p)
phakara (ph)	B *bakara* (b)	*bhakaru* (bh)	M *makara* (m)
Y *yakara* (y)	R *repha* (r)	L *lakara* (l)	V *vakara* (w)
S *sakara* (sh)	S *sakāra* (sh)	S *sakara* (s)	H *hakara* (h)

THAI

The history of the steamy southeast Asian peninsula is as tumultuous and long as it is shrouded in confusion and intrigue. Punctuated by endless wars, unrest, invasions, misalliances, misrule, and colonization, the area that includes Thailand, Laos, Burma, Cambodia, Vietnam, Malaya, the Philippines, and Indonesia seems to have endured its eternal intrusions with remarkable patience and an impressive flow of architecture, sculpture, painting, and literature. Only Thailand, the "land of the free," officially known as Siam, managed to escape outright foreign rule, if not foreign influence, and to maintain her ethnic independence.

Although the gentle, musical Thais are descended from aggressive Mongol tribes who filtered into southeast Asia from China about 100 A.D., Thailand did not become a country until the 1300s, and was unknown to Europeans until the 1500s. During this period, the Thais, like their neighbors, were caught between the explosive political threats of China to the north and the quietly persistent cultural persuasions of India to the west. Not wanting to be eaten by the Chinese dragon or stampeded by the sacred Indian bull, the Thais insured their survival by paying tribute money and goods to the Chinese warlords while praying to the God Buddha of the Indian missionaries. Later, they fended off serious foreign colonization by establishing trade agreements with Holland, England, and France. By the 1850s they had begun to modernize by western standards.

It remained for India, however, without armies, agreements, or threats, to exert the greatest influence on Thailand. And this she did during the thirteenth century by introducing the Thais to writing and the Indian Sanskrit alphabet (see pages 53–55). Schooled in Sanskrit, the Thais were infused with a strong dose of Indian literature and culture. In time, the Thais altered the alphabet to suit their own language, needs, and personality.

consonants			ก K	ข (kh)
ค (kh)	ฆ (kh)	ง (kng)	จ C	ฉ (ch)
ช (ch)	ฌ (ch)	ญ J	ฎ D	ฏ T
ฐ (th)	ฑ (th)	ฒ (th)	ณ N	ด D
ต T	ถ (th)	ท (th)	ธ (th)	น N
บ B	ป P	ผ F	พ F	ภ (ph)
ม M	ย J	ร R	ล L	ศ S

ษ S	ส S	ห H	ฟ H	ฮ H
ว W	vowels		–ะ (ah-ah)	–ั (short ah)
–า (long ah)	–ิ (ih-ih)	–ี (short ih)	–ึ (uh-uh)	–ือ (long uh)
–ุ (ooh-ooh)	–ู (long ooh)	เ–ะ (eh-eh)	เ– (short eh)	แ–ะ (ai-ai)
แ– (long ai)	โ–ะ (oh-oh)	โ– (long oh)	– (short oh)	เ–าะ (aw-aw)
–อ (long aw)	ไ– (short adg)	–าย (long adg)	ใ– (short adg)	เ–า (short ahw)
–าว (long ahw)	ฤ (ruh)	ฤๅ (ruh-uh)	ฦ (luh)	ฦๅ (luh-uh)

TIBETAN

High on a plateau in central Asia, hemmed in by vast mountains, including the soaring Himalayas, sits one of the world's most remote lands, Tibet. Harsh and forbidding, Tibet is surrounded by India, Nepal, Bhutan, Sikkim, Burma, and China. An unwilling province of The People's Republic of China since the 1950s, Tibet still clings to her ancient form of Indian Buddhism, Lamaism, and to the guardians of her traditions, the Dalai and Pachen Lamas, spiritual heads of Lamaism.

The Tibetan language, understandably, is closely related to Indian, Burmese, and Chinese dialects. However, India exerted more influence on Tibet's early social history than did China. Together, these myriad pressures entered Tibet from every direction and probably account for the endless dialects that riddle the Tibetan language. Nearly everyone of the 105 districts in this compact country of three million people — the population of modern Athens, Greece — speaks its own dialect!

The one dialect considered to be correct Tibetan is *Lhasan*, the speech pattern of Lhasa, Tibet's capital city. And the single alphabet of Tibet expresses the Lhasan dialect.

Originally, the letters of the Tibetan alphabet were taken from the Indian Sanskrit Devanagari alphabet (pages 53–55) sometime during the seventh century A.D., although Tibetan word sounds differed from Indian word sounds. The look of the letters changed in response to Tibetan usage and cultural tendencies. In the course of time, Tibet was subjected to strong Chinese influences as reflected in the tapered stroke of the letter design.

Today, the Tibetan alphabet is neither Indian nor Chinese in appearance or representation, however much it recalls both. The alphabet is distinctly Asian and singularly Tibetan.

K (ka)	K (kha)	K (k'a)
(nga)	(cha)	(chha)
(ch'a)	(nya)	T (ta)
T (tha)	T (t'a)	N (na)
P (pa)	P (pha)	P (p'a)
M (ma)	(tsa)	(tsha)

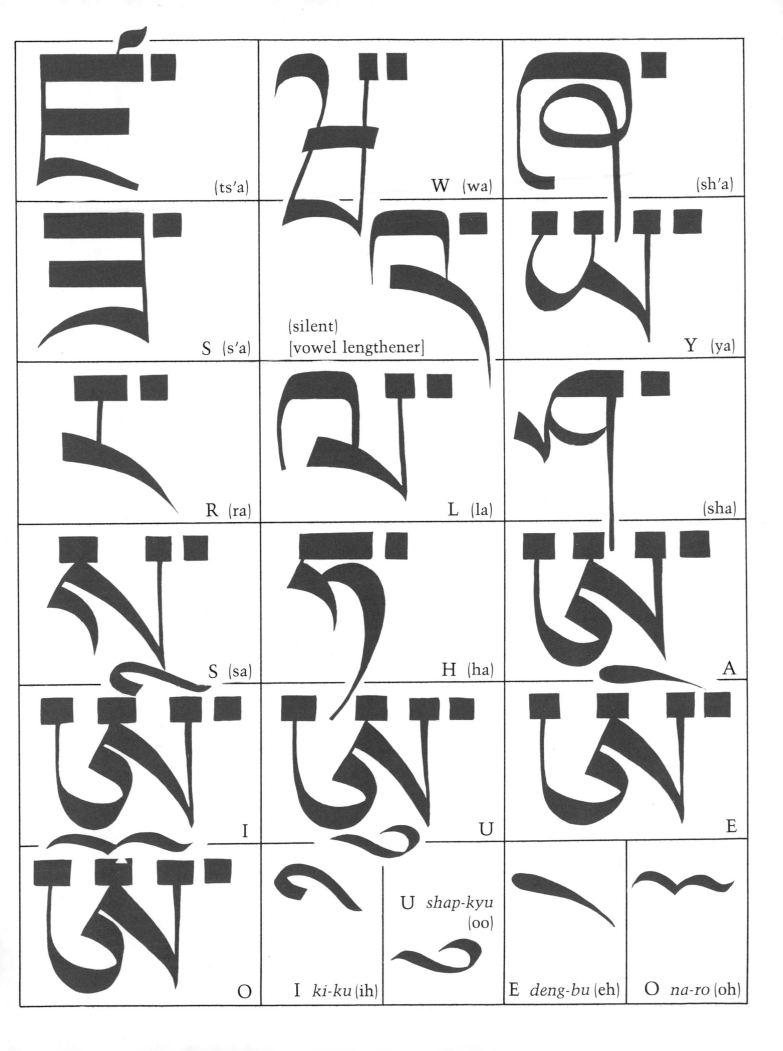

(ts'a)	W (wa)	(sh'a)
S (s'a)	(silent) [vowel lengthener]	Y (ya)
R (ra)	L (la)	(sha)
S (sa)	H (ha)	A
I	U	E
O	I *ki-ku* (ih) — U *shap-kyu* (oo)	E *deng-bu* (eh) — O *na-ro* (oh)

upper left. Tibetan E; *upper right,* Chinese F; *lower left,* Hebrew G; *lower right,* Arabic H

DA